THE STONE FACE

"To be is to be perceived."
—SAMUEL BECKETT, on the meaning of *Film*

"A man may keep away from everybody, but he cannot get away from himself."
—BUSTER KEATON, on the meaning of *Film*

THE STONE FACE

A PLAY BY

Sherry MacDonald

[signature: Sherry MacDonald]

ANVIL PRESS | 2007

Copyright © 2007 by Sherry MacDonald

Anvil Press Publishers Inc.
P.O. Box 3008, Main Post Office
Vancouver, B.C. V6B 3X5 canada
www.anvilpress.com

All rights reserved. No part of this book may be reproduced by any means without the prior written permission of the publisher, with the exception of brief passages in reviews. Any request for photocopying or other reprographic copying of any part of this book must be directed in writing to access: The Canadian Copyright Licensing Agency, One Yonge Street, Suite 800, Toronto, Ontario, Canada, M5E 1E5.

LIBRARY AND ARCHIVES CANADA CATALOGUING IN PUBLICATION

MacDonald, Sherry
    The stone face : a play / Sherry MacDonald.

ISBN 978-1-895636-87-1

1. Film (Motion picture : 1965)—Drama.   2. Schneider, Alan, 1917-1984—Drama.
3. Keaton, Buster, 1895-1966—Drama.   4. Beckett, Samuel, 1906-1989—Drama.   I. Title.

PS8625.D753S76 2007   C812'.6   C2007-906039-0

Printed and bound in Canada
Cover and interior design: HeimatHouse
Author photo: Parjad Sharifi

Represented in Canada by the Literary Press Group
Distributed by the University of Toronto Press

The publisher gratefully acknowledges the financial assistance of the Canada Council for the Arts, the Book Publishing Industry Development Program (BPIDP), and the Province of British Columbia through the B.C. Arts Council and the Book Publishing Tax Credit.

The Stone Face premiered on October 26, 2007 at the Waterfront Theatre in Vancouver, B.C. It was produced by Damfino Theatre with the following cast and crew:

BUSTER	Alex Diakun
ALAN	Allan Zinyk
SAM	Terence Kelly
ELEANOR	Anna Hagan
YOUNG MAN	Kyle Rideout

Directed by	Kevin McKendrick
Set Design by	Yulia Shtern
Lighting Design by	Parjad Sharifi
Costume Design by	Carmen Alatorre
Sound Design by	Ronin Wong
Gag Consultant	Peter Anderson
Assistant Director	Stephanie Plaitin
Technical Director	Craig Alfredson
Stage Manager	Danielle Fecko
Publicist	Andrew Templeton

ACKNOWLEDGMENTS:

The Stone Face first appeared at Playwrights' Theatre Centre in Vancouver on November 25, 2003 and was subsequently presented at the Centre's New Play Festival in May, 2004.

The play was also developed at PlayWorks Ink 2004 with the assistance of the Alberta Playwrights' Network (which receives funding support from Theatre Alberta).

The Stone Face was originally produced in the United States in February 2007 as a Workshop Production of the Harriett Lake Festival of New Plays at the Orlando-UCF Shakespeare Festival. It was directed by Dan McCleary; the stage manager was Seth Payeur. The cast was as follows:

BUSTER . . . . J.D. Sutton
ALAN . . . . Jason Flora
SAM . . . . Bob Lipka
ELEANOR . . . . Jan Wikstrom
YOUNG MAN . . . . Michael Lane

The writing of this play would not have been possible without the generous support of Sylvia MacDonald.

Thank you also to the B.C. Arts Council, the Creative Writing Program at UBC and the UBC film library.

Finally, thank you to the unsuspecting real-life counterparts to the characters in the play: Buster Keaton, Eleanor Norris Keaton, Samuel Beckett, and Alan Schneider for having provided such a wealth of inspiration.

This play is for all artists who dedicate themselves to the serious business of making comedy.

FOREWORD

Alan in Wonderland, or, When is a Gag not a Gag?

The Stone Face by Sherry MacDonald is referenced in the Wikipedia entry on *Film*, the movie project which brought Samuel Beckett, Buster Keaton, and director Alan Schneider together in 1964. Keaton and Beckett are cultural icons, but Schneider is less well-remembered. Buster's first act reading of the high points of his resume is not entirely helpful, although it does remind us that among other career highlights Alan Schneider directed the premiere production of Edward Albee's *Who's Afraid of Virginia Woolf.*

But the Alan of *The Stone Face* seems altogether too innocent and eager to be the man who led the first successful assault on Albee's screaming jungle of a play. In a brave re-imagining, Sherry MacDonald has turned him into an Everyman for the 21st century—a perpetual graduate student, overly confident of his theoretical knowledge, but somewhat lost in the world in which he finds himself—a much closer relative of Beckett's tramps and Keaton's poker-faced heroes than of the actual "Alan Schneider."

From his first entrance, attached to a piece of paper which he cannot seem to get free of, Alan is caught in a silent movie gag. (Does this represent the Beckett script for which he has a virtually slavish devotion?) He is drawn into the topsy-turvy world of Buster Keaton, into a maze of sticky paper, dubious drinks, mimed surfaces which unaccountably prove solid and, most importantly, into a vociferous card game between the silent movie legend and his long-dead colleagues.

But *The Stone Face* offers much more than a heady combination of 1965 French Absurdism and the comic world of classic silent comedy which was also being rediscovered at the time—posters of the young, pale-faced, and very beautiful Buster Keaton were as ubiquitous as bean bag chairs in pads across North America—for Sherry MacDonald has crafted Alan's path to enlightenment along lines which relate more to the training of a Zen adept. As is the custom, Keaton, the master, speaks in dry aphorisms—"You have to be able to play. Otherwise the game's gonna go on without you."—while at the same time catching

Alan up in a hilarious series of gags—metaphorical life lessons with all the knotted difficulty and buried wisdom of Zen koans.

To give but one example, Alan's attempts to elucidate the action of *Film* lead him into a stripped down variation on the classic Abbott and Costello routine, "Who's on First?"

ALAN: E, who is, of course, the subject, the one doing the observing. P.O.V. camera.
ELEANOR: Oh.
BUSTER: No, E.
ALAN: Yes. E. For "eye."
ELEANOR: Oh. I?
ALAN: Yes.
ELEANOR: I'm sorry, I thought you said E.
ALAN: No. Not I. Eye…

The seemingly disinterested Buster and Sam pursue a game of double solitaire throughout. At one point, Sam offers Alan a somewhat condescending, "Carry on, Alan. You're doing a bang-up job there." But they both exhibit the proverbial master's lack of interest in a student who is more than clever at talking the talk but has, as yet, no idea of how to walk the walk. Alan's climactic statement that "the object must reinvent himself in accordance with the discovery of the subject, become a participant as well as an observer,"—which is surely the precise personal challenge which he seems determined not to see—is answered by Buster's laconic, "I think I'll do the fish now," as he goes off to prepare the barbecue.

And then there's the great Red Skelton gag that proves Alan's final test. Red attempts to escape from a house whose door is guarded by a ferocious dog—to literally "get out of the box." Alan can't figure out how Red's going to do it, and it's unlikely that we will either. Throughout the second act, it works on our minds with a kind of gnarled thorniness. Obviously there's an answer and Alan just can't get it. But that's not really the point. He's become involved, hopelessly involved, in the attempt to solve the puzzle. He's learning to play the game, and we, engrossed in Sherry MacDonald's witty ability to turn gags into metaphors, are playing along with him.

—M<small>ARTIN</small> K<small>INCH</small>, *Executive Director*
Playwrights Theatre Centre, Vancouver, B.C.

Characters

Buster: Sixty or so years old, silent film comedy star
Alan: Early to mid-forties, New York theatre director
Eleanor: Fifties, former dancer, Buster's wife
Sam: Around sixty, award-winning writer
Young Man: Twenties, Buster Keaton screen persona

Setting

The year is 1964.

Act One
The home of Buster and Eleanor in California.

Act Two
Scenes One and Two: The set of *Film*, New York City.
Scene Three: *Film*, projector and projected, a suspension of time and place.
Scene Four: Outside the entrance to a cinema, New York Film Festival.

Design

The design shall not employ screen projections of any silent film, be they Keaton films or *Film* itself, or any other film. In a sense, the play is the film, even becoming *Film* at one point, and should not be laid out open for any sort of comparison to the "real" thing, which will only serve as a distraction, rather than an enhancement.

Music from the silent film era may be employed as seen fit. If desired, music can bleed into any of the scenes, with the exception of Act Two, Scene Three, which must be performed in complete silence (with the possible exception of the "whir" of a film projector, if need be).

Scene changes may take on a filmic quality, with the possibility of the Young Man "conducting" and/or participating in the action of the scene change.

ACT ONE

SCENE ONE

The year is 1964. BUSTER*'s living room.*

The YOUNG MAN *enters from the parlour, straightening and cleaning. He pulls out a handkerchief and begins to dust. He sees some papers lying about and begins to tidy them. One of the papers sticks to his hand. He removes the paper. It sticks to his other hand.*

The doorbell rings.

Putting his hand to the ground, he steps on the paper with his shoe, whereupon it becomes stuck. He steps on the paper with his other shoe. It becomes stuck to that shoe now instead.

The doorbell rings again.

He looks around for somewhere to unstick the paper but can't figure it out.

ALAN: *(from off)* Hello?

The YOUNG MAN *stands by the entrance and puts out his foot,*

THE STONE FACE

waiting. **ALAN** *enters. He steps on the paper. It becomes stuck to* **ALAN**'*s shoe now instead.*

ALAN: I rang the bell but no one answered. I—

The **YOUNG MAN** *exits to the parlour.*

ALAN *notices the paper stuck to his shoe. He removes it and it sticks to his hand.* **ALAN** *removes the paper, but it sticks to his other hand. Frustrated, he shakes his hand trying to remove the paper.*

The **YOUNG MAN** *enters again, carrying a toolkit and a framed photograph of a young Buster Keaton.*

ALAN: I seem to have . . . I'm looking for Mr. Keaton.

The **YOUNG MAN** *holds out the photo for* **ALAN**, *who takes it.* **THE YOUNG MAN** *puts the toolkit down, takes out a hammer and hammers a nail to the wall. He then takes the photo from* **ALAN** *and hangs it up. The paper is now stuck to the back of the photo. The* **YOUNG MAN** *takes out a handkerchief and dusts the photo.* **ALAN** *looks at the photo curiously. The* **YOUNG MAN** *offers to take* **ALAN**'*s coat.*

ALAN: Thank you.

The removal of **ALAN**'*s coat becomes a sight gag where* **ALAN** *tries to take his arm out of his sleeve, only to have the* **YOUNG MAN** *circle around, making it quite difficult to remove the coat.*
  The **YOUNG MAN** *is finally able to remove the coat. However, with the* **YOUNG MAN** *having circled about once again,* **ALAN** *ends up with the coat back on.* **ALAN** *removes his own coat. The* **YOUNG MAN** *takes the coat and hangs it on the coat rack. The* **YOUNG MAN** *offers a chair to* **ALAN**.

ALAN: Thank you. I have an appointment.

The **YOUNG MAN** *gets his handkerchief out again and begins to dust and polish.*

ACT ONE

ALAN: Is he in?

The **YOUNG MAN** *nods "yes."*

ALAN: Will he be coming out?

The **YOUNG MAN** *nods "yes" again.*

ALAN *watches as the* **YOUNG MAN** *polishes the glass casing on the face of a grandfather clock. The* **YOUNG MAN** *pulls out a pocket watch and checks the time. Seeing the time is not right, he adjusts the hands of the clock by putting his finger straight through the "glass," which, in fact, doesn't exist. The* **YOUNG MAN** *stands back to admire his work, tips his hat to* **ALAN** *and, picking up his toolkit, exits through the parlour door.* **ALAN** *walks over to the clock to take a closer look.* **BUSTER** *enters from the parlour, a cigarette dangling from his lips and cards in his hand.*

BUSTER: Eight trumps! Can you believe it?
ALAN: Ah, Mr. Keaton.
BUSTER: I've been waitin' for this moment. Bam! Just to see the look on his face. It's bridge tonight. The secret's in the partnering.
ALAN: I imagine—
BUSTER: *(shouting towards the parlour)* Thalberg! Used to partner with him. *(shouting again)* Till he cheated me! Owes me close to two million dollars. Rides on credit. *(shouting)* Cheap bastard! Schneider, isn't it?

BUSTER *extends his hand, which* **ALAN** *shakes.*

ALAN: Alan.
BUSTER: Make yourself at home, Alan. I won't be long.

BUSTER *exits to the parlour, leaving* **ALAN** *alone. He looks again at the photo.* **BUSTER** *enters from the parlour, still holding his cards.*

BUSTER: Hard Luck.

THE STONE FACE

ALAN: Beg your pardon?
BUSTER: A still from one of my films: *Hard Luck*.
ALAN: Oh. Yes. Mr. Keaton, I wanted to ask you, there was a young man just here. He looks an awful lot like—do you have a son?
BUSTER: I have two sons.
ALAN: I thought it might be the case.
BUSTER: I haven't hardly seen 'em in years. It's the Talmadge influence. My first wife and her sisters. Poisoned them against me.
ALAN: I'm sorry. It's . . . the young man. This photo.
BUSTER: Would you excuse me?

BUSTER exits back into the parlour.

BUSTER: (*off, shouting*) Goddamn you, Joe! This is the last time I partner with you. I swear to god!

ALAN goes towards the parlour. Just as he reaches the parlour door, BUSTER enters with a drink for ALAN.

BUSTER: Drink? Hope you don't mind bourbon. I'm out of scotch. And scotch, even a cheap scotch, is always better than even the best bourbon. Cheers.

BUSTER and ALAN both take a drink. ALAN displays an odd face.

BUSTER: Cornwater to be sure. But it's all we got.
ALAN: If this is a bad time—
BUSTER: Not at all.
ALAN: What about your guests?
BUSTER: They're all right. They have sandwiches.
ALAN: It sounds quite . . . hostile.
BUSTER: This is nothing. You should see it on poker night.
ALAN: What happens then?
BUSTER: Let's just say Eleanor makes sure to hide the sharp utensils on poker night. Care to join us?
ALAN: (*alarmed at the prospect*) No. Thank you.
BUSTER: Are you sure?

ACT ONE

ALAN: Yes.
BUSTER: You do play?
ALAN: Uh . . . no.
BUSTER: Maybe not bridge, but surely poker. There's a secret to that too.
ALAN: I'm afraid I don't play cards.
BUSTER: What do you mean you don't play cards? You have to play. Otherwise the game's gonna go on without you. It's in the face, you know.
ALAN: How's that?
BUSTER: The secret to poker. Have to keep the face still. Not give anything away. Even the eyes.
ALAN: Uh . . . Mr. Keaton . . .
BUSTER: Call me Buster.
ALAN: Buster . . .
BUSTER: Never used to be a name. Buster. A buster was a knock on the chin or on the head. You say, "that fella took a real buster." A lump on the head, a wallop-like. It was Harry Houdini who gave me the name. The Three Keatons—we were on the same bill as him in The Traveling Medicine Show. I was six months old when I took a tumble down a flight of stairs. Houdini takes one look at me and says, "That's some buster you took there." And the name stuck.
ALAN: I see.
BUSTER: Even (*shouting*) Thalberg! is impressed with that story.
ALAN: Buster . . . didn't we have a conversation today?
BUSTER: We're having a conversation right now.
ALAN: I mean on the telephone. We made an appointment for eight o'clock.
BUSTER: Yeah. It's eight now. Or ten after, according to my clock. Except you can never be too sure with this clock. It was a gift from the Marx Brothers. A bonus for helping them solve a problem with one of their gags. Harpo had to get a mattress from one room to another without being seen. They were all worked up over the missing door.
ALAN: The missing—?
BUSTER: It was already established so there was no going back. It occurred to me instead of fretting over the mattress, our best bet was to draw attention to it. So I had Harpo hold it up in plain

15

view. The other characters were right there. That's what made it work so well.

ALAN: Mr. Keaton . . .

BUSTER: The best part's coming up. Harpo held up the mattress while the other guys walked past. Harpo turned around behind the mattress and backed out, holding it out in front. They could see it and at the same time, they couldn't. See?

ALAN: No.

BUSTER: Don't worry. You will.

ALAN: Uh . . . Buster. I wanted to meet with you tonight. Prior to meeting with Sam. See if you had any questions.

BUSTER: Does Mr. Beckett like barbecues?

ALAN: Barbecues?

BUSTER: Barbecues.

ALAN: I don't know. We never discussed barbecues.

BUSTER: You haven't? Hmmm . . . interesting. See I was thinking about having a barbecue tomorrow. Takes the pressure off of Eleanor.

ALAN: Oh. I see. Yes. A barbecue will be fine.

BUSTER: You'll like my wife. Used to be a dancer. Performed as part of my act in Paris right after we were married. The French love us. Too bad about the bourbon though.

ALAN: Uh . . . look . . . maybe we should resume this meeting tomorrow. With Sam.

BUSTER: Not at all. Not at all. This script you sent me. It's very interesting. What were you thinking of calling it?

ALAN: Calling it?

BUSTER: The title.

ALAN: It has a title. It's called *Film*.

BUSTER *looks at the script.*

BUSTER: Oh. I didn't realize that was the title. The film is called *Film*?

ALAN: Yes.

BUSTER: Isn't that like calling a dog, *Dog*?

ALAN: No. That's not an accurate analogy at all. Calling the film Film is rather a stroke of genius—Sam's, not mine, of course. You see, while the film—

ACT ONE

Buster: Film.
Alan: Yes. The film, *Film*, is about the object versus the subject. Titling the film simply *Film*, in effect draws attention to the subject as a reflection of its viewed self.

A long pause.

Alan: To be is to be perceived. Sam's words.

Pause.

Alan: Each element of the film—
Buster: *Film.*
Alan: Yes. Each element of the film—including the title—is meticulously drawn out. Sam has a very specific statement he wants to make.
Buster: I wish you'd let me know what it is.
Alan: Yes. Well. A Beckett work can be challenging.
Buster: Don't worry. We'll have this thing in shape in no time. I've got some great ideas for gags. Fill in some of this dead space.
Alan: Dead space?
Buster: Yeah. It's not gonna be a problem, though. You put me in an empty room with nothing more than a broom and I could fill up a good two reels, maybe more. Take *Candid Camera*. All's I had to do is sit down at a lunch counter. An ordinary coffee and donut shop and I could have the whole place in stitches. It's amazing what you can do with a bowl of soup and a pair of glasses.
Alan: You don't understand—
Buster: Take this stone wall sequence here at the beginning. I could do a bit where it seems like I'm holding the wall up on my own, lean in at an extreme angle. It's an old trick—
Alan: It's not that kind of film.
Buster: Padding is what we used to call it.
Alan: Padding! Buster . . . Mr. Keaton.
Buster: Yeah?

Short beat.

THE STONE FACE

ALAN: We don't pad Beckett.

Pause.

ALAN: This project is very important. This is Beckett's premiere foray into celluloid.

BUSTER: Did you know Salvador Dali wore a turn of the century underwater diving suit when giving a lecture on Surrealism at the Museum of Modern Art? It was to open the World's Fair. His way of paying tribute to the underwater sequence I performed in *The Navigator*. It was when he unveiled his famous lobster telephone.

ALAN: Mr. Keaton . . .

BUSTER: I could've gotten into the picture business a lot sooner, but my father. He was having none of it. "You want to put The Three Keatons on a bed sheet and have people pay a nickel to see us? No thank you." It was Roscoe, Roscoe Arbuckle—you probably know him as "Fatty." He taught me everything about making pictures. Gave me my first film. *The Butcher Boy*.

ALAN: Buster, I know you've had a very successful—

BUSTER: Timing. That's the ticket. Roscoe taught me that. "I got my back turned." I says to him. "How am I gonna keep from flinching when you throw that sacka flour if my back is turned?" "Don't worry," he says. "Turn around when I say. It'll be there." And it was. Knocked me ass over tea kettle. My feet were up where my head should be. And my head was down where my feet should be.

ALAN: Buster. You've made many films. Many great films. Your contribution to the art of filmmaking is enormous.

Beat.

ALAN: But this is nineteen sixty-four. Things are . . . different.

BUSTER: Uh huh . . . Seems to me I was to play another one of Mr. Beckett's characters. For a play. A few years ago.

ALAN: That's right.

BUSTER: Something with a dog's name.

ACT ONE

Pause.

ALAN: You mean . . . Lucky?
BUSTER: Yeah. What was that thing called? *Waiting For . . . Waiting For . . .*
ALAN: Buster . . .
BUSTER: No. That wasn't it. Don't worry, it'll come to me.

BUSTER *exits.*

BUSTER: *(from off)* You lost this round! Yes, you did! You get back in that game now! I said, get back!

Smacking and whimpering sounds are heard, followed by a loud crash. **ALAN** *goes to open the door, but can't. The door is stuck.* **BUSTER** *reenters, with a plate of sandwiches.*

BUSTER: *Godot!*

ALAN *just looks at* **BUSTER.**

BUSTER: Sandwich?

A moment passes.

ALAN: You're having a good time, aren't you?
BUSTER: I am. Thank you for asking.
ALAN: The reason I came tonight is because I wanted to make sure everything was . . . okay.

Pause.

ALAN: I know things have been a little difficult for you and . . .

Pause.

BUSTER: Tell me, Schneider, have you seen any of my pictures?
ALAN: That's not really the issue here. I—

19

BUSTER: This is your first time directing a film, isn't it?

ALAN: I've directed for the stage many times . . .

BUSTER *waits.*

ALAN: Yes. It's my first film.

BUSTER: When you sent me the script, you said Mr. Beckett wanted me for the role.

ALAN: Yes. I thought it wise to have a meeting with you first. He doesn't know you.

BUSTER: But he does want me.

Pause.

ALAN: The first film of yours I saw was *Sherlock Jr.* What made the film revolutionary of course was its use of editing. A comment on the very act of filmmaking. What I remember about it is the young man, falling asleep in the projection booth. And then entering right into the film.

Pause.

ALAN: I do know your work, Mr. Keaton. I've seen several of your films. I saw *The General* twice and I absolutely agree with the best assessments of that landmark film: it was truly a work of genius.

ALAN *takes one of the sandwiches.*

ALAN: In it's time.

ALAN *takes a bite of his sandwich.*

BUSTER: Alan Schneider. Director of works by writers such as Thornton Wilder, Edward Albee, Clifford Odets, and . . . Samuel Beckett. Career highlights include the 1962 world premiere of *Who's Afraid of Virginia Woolf.* Described in *The New York Times* as "A wry and electric evening in the theatre." The *Times* also stated

ACT ONE

"Mr. Schneider is one of the finest directors to be found on the American . . .

BUSTER *picks up a sandwich.*

BUSTER: . . . stage."

BUSTER *takes a bite of the sandwich. Having reached a kind of stalemate,* **BUSTER** *and* **ALAN** *eat their sandwiches.*

ALAN: Things seem pretty quiet in there. The card game.
BUSTER: They do settle down. If you leave them be.
ALAN: Thalberg, huh?
BUSTER: Yeah.
ALAN: Irving G. Thalberg?
BUSTER: Yes.
ALAN: The Irving G. Thalberg who died thirty years ago?

Pause.

BUSTER: I'll get your coat.

BUSTER *retrieves* **ALAN***'s coat.* **ALAN** *looks once again at the photo.*

ALAN: When was this picture taken?
BUSTER: Nineteen twenty-one.
ALAN: Who was the young man that was here before?
BUSTER: Young man?
  ALAN *wanders over to the clock.*
ALAN: He was here, polishing and cleaning.
BUSTER: Ah . . .
ALAN: Who was he?
BUSTER: Someone I used to know.

ALAN *reaches out to touch the clock. He attempts to put his finger through the glass, but can't.* **BUSTER** *holds out* **ALAN***'s coat.*

21

THE STONE FACE

He performs a similar coat gag to the one performed earlier.

ALAN: Thank you.
BUSTER: You sure you don't play cards?
ALAN: I'm sure.
BUSTER: We'll have to fix that, I think.

Blackout.
End of Scene One.

SCENE TWO

The next day. **BUSTER**'s *living room.* **ELEANOR** *lies on the floor, eyes closed.*

BUSTER: *(from off)* I hope you like fish.
ALAN: *(from off)* Oh. Yes.
BUSTER: *(from off)* I wish I could say I caught it myself but I'm afraid I'm not much of a fisherman. Don't like boats. Can't trust 'em. Too many funny things happen on 'em. Can I get you a drink?

BUSTER enters from the front door area, a cigarette dangling from his lips. He crosses towards the parlour.

BUSTER: Don't worry. It's scotch.

BUSTER exits to the parlour. **ALAN** *enters and sees* **ELEANOR** *on the floor. He moves towards her.* **BUSTER** *emerges from the parlour with two drinks. He hands one to* **ALAN**.

BUSTER: I cut it with water. I hope that's okay.
ALAN: Buster . . .
BUSTER: Oh. I see you've met my wife. It's the bourbon. Nasty stuff. She does this all the time. It's almost a routine. Don't worry. I'll take care of it.

ACT ONE

BUSTER *exits to the parlour.* **ALAN** *takes another close look at* **ELEANOR**, *who is still completely passed out. Alan takes a drink and makes the same face as he did earlier with the bourbon. The* **YOUNG MAN** *enters. He begins to dust. The* **YOUNG MAN** *dusts the coat rack. Bending over, he catches his hat on the coat rack. He turns, sees* **ELEANOR**, *goes over to her, scratches his head. He notices his hat is missing. Looks around for it, confused.*
   He exits.
   BUSTER *enters from the parlour, dragging a folding lounge chair. With great effort, he drags the chair into the living room.* **BUSTER** *tries to set up the folding chair, but it's not cooperative. It folds back in on itself.* **BUSTER** *sets up the chair again. It continues to give him some problems which he finally overcomes. Once the chair is set up,* **BUSTER** *pulls the dead-weight* **ELEANOR** *up and into the chair. This requires a few repeated efforts. Once* **BUSTER** *gets* **ELEANOR** *into the chair, it folds in on her. He tries to straighten it out, but the bottom folds up. Finally,* **BUSTER** *straightens out the chair with* **ELEANOR** *in it. He drags the chair out and into the parlour, closing the door behind him.*
   Without missing a beat, **ELEANOR** *enters. She is in the best of spirits. She carries a tray of crackers and cheese.*

ELEANOR: You must be Alan. So nice to meet you. Cheese?
ALAN: Uh no . . . no, thank you. That was very good. You played your part very convincingly.

ELEANOR *smiles, not understanding.*

ALAN: Your husband had me going yesterday as well for a while.
ELEANOR: Oh?
ALAN: Cards.
ELEANOR: Oh, yes. Cards. It's how Buster and I met: cards. I was a dancer on contract at MGM and us kids were always playing: pinochle, poker, bridge. Floyd Nelson—he was one of the boy dancers, but that's another story. Floyd told me about a place where there was always a bridge game going on all day, every day and a good teacher to boot. As it turned out, the bridge game was

at Buster's house and the good teacher was Buster. People were always coming and going. Real crack players. Now I knew who Buster was. But even though I was a pretty young thing—just a girl, really. As far as Buster was concerned, I was just a pair a hands holding cards. 'Til one day someone yelled at me for playing a wrong card and I got angry and yelled right back. It was the first time Buster noticed me.

BUSTER *enters.*

BUSTER: Eleanor. That bourbon. You knew we were expecting guests.
ELEANOR: I'm sorry.
BUSTER: I'm glad Mr. Beckett wasn't here to see that.
ELEANOR: Where is Mr. Beckett?
ALAN: He had an appointment. He'll be along. Told me to come on ahead, he was going to take a taxi. Except I'm not sure if it was the best idea.
ELEANOR: Why?
ALAN: Sam has a terrible fear of traffic. It's his first time in the United States. And he has a terrible fear of anything relating to North American cities.
ELEANOR: What a shame. I hope we'll be able to make him feel at home. Both of you.
ALAN: Thank you, Mrs. Keaton.
ELEANOR: Call me Eleanor.
ALAN: Eleanor.

BUSTER *pulls out a pencil and a pad of paper from his pocket. He writes something on the paper, presumably to set up a score sheet of some kind. The pencil breaks. He pulls out a sharpener from his pocket and begins to sharpen the pencil.*

ELEANOR: So. Alan. Buster tells me you are a very accomplished theatre director.
ALAN: I've had my share of good luck.
ELEANOR: Surely it's more than luck.
ALAN: I suppose . . .

ACT ONE

ALAN *takes note of the extreme pencil-sharpening.*

ALAN: I try to do the material justice, wherever I can . . .
ELEANOR: Come now. No need to be modest. You're among friends.
ALAN: Thank you, Mrs. Keaton—Eleanor—I have been fortunate to work with some very good writers.
ELEANOR: They wouldn't trust you if they didn't think you were up to it.
ALAN: It's nice of you to say.
ELEANOR: Just giving credit where credit is due.
ALAN: Thank you.

BUSTER, *finally satisfied with the sharpness of the pencil, writes something on the pad of paper. The pencil breaks and he has to start all over again. He begins to sharpen it once more.*

ELEANOR: Must be a fine place to work. The theatre.
ALAN: I have no complaints. *(beat)* Of course, I have complaints—
ELEANOR: Oh?
ALAN: No, I . . . no. No complaints.
ELEANOR: Oh. That's nice. Ritz?
ALAN: No. Thanks.

Pause. **ALAN** *glances over at Buster, who is still busy sharpening his pencil.*

ELEANOR: Theatre, huh?
ALAN: Yes. I've worked in television.
ELEANOR: Oh. Television. Buster's done television. He even had his own show.
ALAN: I didn't know.
ELEANOR: Oh yes. He likes television. But having his own show didn't agree with him. There wasn't enough time to perfect the routines as far as Buster was concerned. He's such a perfectionist.

ALAN *looks at* **BUSTER** *whose pencil-sharpening is causing long shavings to fall all around him.*

THE STONE FACE

ALAN: Your husband and I have that in common then. Can almost get me in trouble sometimes.
ELEANOR: Oh?
ALAN: I didn't mean—No. No trouble.
ELEANOR: Oh. That's nice.

ALAN looks over to BUSTER, who, finally satisfied with the sharpness of the pencil, holds it up for full viewing. The pencil is now ridiculously short.

ELEANOR: Your first film: *Film*.
ALAN: How's that?
ELEANOR: *Film*. It's your first film.
ALAN: Yes. Uh . . . Eleanor. It's important that you know—both of you—I have a strong desire to do justice to Sam's vision. My relationship with Sam is very important. I wouldn't do anything to jeopardize it.

BUSTER begins to write with the pencil, but has trouble because it is too short.

ELEANOR: Would you say you fear him?
ALAN: No. I didn't mean—
ELEANOR: Perhaps I should talk to him for you. I'm very good at smoothing out relationships.
ALAN: It's not necessary. Believe me.
ELEANOR: Alan, I know it must be difficult for you to stand up to Mr. Beckett.
ALAN: I promise you, Mrs. Keaton, I don't feel the need to stand up to Mr. Beckett—I mean, Sam.
ELEANOR: Fear is such a debilitating thing. Are you sure you don't want any cheese?
ALAN: No. Thank you.
ELEANOR: Try the gouda. I bought it fresh this morning.

BUSTER, having finally given up on the small pencil, removes a second pencil from his pocket and begins to sharpen it now.

ACT ONE

ALAN: Mrs. Keaton—
ELEANOR: Uh, uh. Eleanor.
ALAN: Eleanor. Sam's always trusted me enough to give me full reign—I wouldn't actually take full reign. Of course I consult Sam most often. Quite meticulously. On most every point. I do so because it is what's best for the project. I do so out of choice. Not because I am bound by the writer. I am my own person.
ELEANOR: Yes, I see. Gherkin?
ALAN: No. Thank you.
ELEANOR: I know what you're saying, Alan. You are dealing with a genius. Believe me, I sympathize with your position completely.

ALAN looks over at BUSTER who continues to sharpen the pencil.

ALAN: Let me assure you. Sam and I are in complete synchronization. We've worked together on all his plays.
ELEANOR: In Europe?
ALAN: No. Here in America.
ELEANOR: I don't understand. I thought you said this was Mr. Beckett's first visit to America.
ALAN: Well . . . we haven't exactly worked together. We've had several in-person meetings, of course, and numerous correspondences. But in terms of the work, mostly I provide him with updates and he gives me notes by way of letter or telegram. That kind of thing.
ELEANOR: So this will be the first time the two of you work on a project together. At the same time. In the same room.

BUSTER stops what he is doing and both he and ELEANOR look at each other. ALAN helps himself to the cheese and crackers.
ELEANOR passes the dish of gherkins to ALAN. He takes one.
BUSTER resumes the sharpening of his pencil.

ELEANOR: Now I know Mr. Beckett's work is beyond criticism.
ALAN: I didn't say that. The script is brilliant, of course. But, as in anything, there could always be room for some minor adjustment.
ELEANOR: Oh?
ALAN: Here or there.

THE STONE FACE

ELEANOR: Where exactly?
ALAN: Nowhere. I'm speaking hypothetically.
ELEANOR: Alan, all conversation is hypothetical. Tell me, where would you make those adjustments?
BUSTER: The wall.
ELEANOR: Oh, the wall. Buster's told you, I think, about the wall.
ALAN: Eleanor, I appreciate your input—
ELEANOR: Oh no. This is Buster's game. I'm only the back-up player.
ALAN: I think you're more than that.
ELEANOR: I do have to look out for Buster's best interests. Much like you look out for Mr. Beckett's.

ALAN notices BUSTER has broken his pencil again. He offers him one of his pens. BUSTER writes something on the paper, presumably a score sheet of some kind, in preparation for playing solitaire. He will shortly begin to lay out cards and play.

ELEANOR: We are agents for the truly gifted, you and I. It's an honourable position.

Pause.

ELEANOR: When Buster told everyone we were getting married, they gathered around: Buster's family, his sister Louise, his doctor, his agent. They sat me down and listed all the reasons why I shouldn't go and tangle myself up with Buster. But I knew. It wasn't that they were trying to protect me from him. It was the other way around. Buster had had enough problems. He didn't need me—some showbiz dame—to cause him any more trouble. I was raised to be a polite girl. So I listened carefully, thanked them for their concerns and then Buster and I went out and got married as planned. Of course, it occurred to me later that what they were really doing was testing me. Seeing whether I could withstand the pressure or whether I'd fold at the first sign of trouble.
ALAN: When I started out in this business I would have done anything to get work. I sent letters out to every theatre producer in town begging them for work. Any work at all. Office work if need be.

ACT ONE

I thought if I could just get my foot in the door. I sent letters to every producer there was. I offered them fifty percent of everything I would ever earn in the theatre or elsewhere—for the rest of my life. If they'd just give me a job. I don't fold easily.
ELEANOR: I'm sure you don't, Alan. Only . . . Buster's had a lot of disappointments.
ALAN: Eleanor. The first time I met Sam was to discuss *Waiting for Godot*, which I was directing in America. He told me in advance he only had half an hour and even *that* he was granting under extreme duress. My notepad in one hand and a bottle of Lacrima Cristi champagne in the other, I met Sam in the lobby of the Lancaster Hotel. My first question was, "Who or what is Godot?" To which he only said, "The play is about two people who are like that. That is all." I put away my note pad and brought out the bottle of champagne. Things improved after that. We ended up spending the better part of ten days together, during which time he took me to London to see a version of *Godot* at the Criterion Theatre where he clutched intermittently at my sleeve and gasped phrases like "He's got it ahl wrahng." And went on to tell me why. At which point I retrieved my notepad and took down every word. (*beat*) Like I said, Sam has yet to come out to America for any of his plays. But he's come for this.

ALAN *picks up the cheese tray and offers some cheese to* **ELEANOR**.

ALAN: I don't plan on disappointing anyone.

She takes a piece of cheese. And a gherkin.
ELEANOR: All right then, Alan.

Pause.

BUSTER: Is he coming?
ALAN: What's that? Oh, you mean Sam. Yes. He's coming.
ELEANOR: Buster's anxious to light the barbecue.
ALAN: I see.
ELEANOR: Maybe you should wait, Buster. After all, we don't want a

THE STONE FACE

barbecue burning away, waiting for Mr. Beckett. What do you think, Alan?

ALAN: I'm sure you're right.

ELEANOR: We'll wait, then.

They wait.

The **YOUNG MAN** *enters, looking about the room, presumably for his hat.* **ALAN** *is the only one who notices him. The* **YOUNG MAN** *goes to the coat rack, bending down to continue his search. He stands, and as he does, the hat, unbeknownst to the* **YOUNG MAN**, *unhooks from the coat rack and onto his head. The* **YOUNG MAN** *is puzzled as to where his hat could be. He bends down again and the hat unhooks once again. With the hat remaining on the hook of the coat rack, the* **YOUNG MAN** *exits, still confused.*

ELEANOR: Another drink?

ALAN: What's that? Oh . . . uh . . . no. Thank you.

ELEANOR: Can't say I blame you.

ALAN: Yes. I don't like to be rude, but is there something wrong with the scotch?

ELEANOR: Nothing wrong with the scotch. Except it's not bourbon.

ALAN: Now that you mention it . . . the bourbon too. They both taste like cold tea.

ELEANOR: Because it is cold tea.

ALAN: Why would you drink it if it's cold tea?

ELEANOR: We do what we have to do.

Pause.

ELEANOR: Maybe you should light the barbecue, Buster. Have it ready for when Mr. Beckett arrives.

BUSTER *nods and stands.*

ELEANOR: Unless … he is coming?

ACT ONE

BUSTER *awaits a reply.*

ALAN: He's coming.

ELEANOR: Maybe you shouldn't light the barbecue quite yet. You do have your card game. Or I could light the barbecue.

ELEANOR *stands.*

ELEANOR: Yes. That's it. I'll light the barbecue. You stay and finish your game.

BUSTER *sits.*

ELEANOR: Or . . . we could both light the barbecue.

BUSTER *stands.*

ELEANOR: Let's both light the barbecue.

Pause.

BUSTER: Shall we go light the barbecue?
ELEANOR: Yes. Let's go light the barbecue.

Neither of them moves. Pause. The **YOUNG MAN** *returns, picks up his hat and exits.* **ALAN** *watches* **BUSTER** *and* **ELEANOR** *who are still standing motionless.*

Pause for another beat.

Blackout.
End of Scene Two.

THE STONE FACE

Scene Three

BUSTER *is alone on stage, playing cards. The others are just off.*

SAM: *(from off)* It was nothing short of a holy bloody nightmare. The criss-cross of highways leading up here. It's like the life and death version of snakes and ladders. Got caught on some sort of loop-de-loop contraption. The cab driver went around in so many circles I thought I was going to vomit. I asked him to slow down. It was like I'd waved a red flag in his face. I could swear the man was foaming at the mouth by the time we arrived.

SAM *enters, followed by* ELEANOR *and* ALAN.

SAM: Tell me, does everyone in this country drive that way, or is it only the ones getting paid?
ELEANOR: I'm sorry your trip was so unsettling, Mr. Beckett.
ALAN: You're all right now though, I hope.
SAM: I survived.
ELEANOR: I understand what you mean about Los Angeles. It's why we moved out of the city.
SAM: Yes, you have a nice little packet of property up here. Away from the stifling madness of the big city. Los Angeles. It's a hiccup away from an institution for the criminally insane.
ELEANOR: Can I help you with your coat?
SAM: Oh no. I know how these coat things end up.
ELEANOR: You'll take a drink though, I hope.
SAM: Scotch, if you have it.
ALAN: I don't think you want a scotch.
SAM: What did you say? Don't want a scotch? Nonsense. I look forward to a decent drink. That dishwater they pedal at the hotel. I may as well be drinking tea.

ELEANOR *exits to the parlour.* SAM *meanders over to* BUSTER*'s cards, takes a look.*

ACT ONE

Alan: Buster. Sam. I am honoured to be given the opportunity to introduce you to one another. Before I do, I'd like to take this moment to ponder the implications of the collaboration ahead of us. The creation of this film—
Sam: Black eight.
Alan: How's that?
Sam: Black eight.
Buster: Oh. Thanks.
Alan: When you think of the significant contribution this collaboration could make to cinematic history—
Sam: I have a deck on me if you'd care to play double.
Buster: Good idea.
Sam: Always be prepared.

Sam pulls out a deck of cards. Buster picks up his cards and shuffles them. Eleanor enters with the drinks.

Eleanor: Cocktails, gentlemen.
Sam: Praise be to god, is there nothing more welcome than the sight of a woman bearing whiskey.
Eleanor: It is my best look. Three fingers. I hope I didn't over pour.
Sam: Not possible. *L'chaim!*

They toast and drink. Alan waits for Sam's reaction. Sam puts his head back and closes his eyes.

Sam: Now that's scotch.
Alan: Tastes all right, does it?
Sam: Nothing like it.

Sam shuffles his cards.

Eleanor: Mr. Beckett—
Sam: You must call me Sam, Mrs. Keaton.
Eleanor: Oh. Eleanor.
Sam: Eleanor.
Eleanor: Sam. I wanted to be sure, before we go any further, to

express to you just how capable I think Alan is. I have every confidence in his abilities.

SAM: We are certainly in agreement there. Alan has directed all my work for the American stage. There's no one I trust more to direct this film.

ELEANOR: Coming from you, those are indeed words of praise.

SAM: The thing about Alan is—and he's totally unaware he's doing it—he doesn't only interpret the words. He literally constructs the space allowing them to exist in a manner that wouldn't be possible otherwise. Like a carpenter might construct an edifice.

ELEANOR: I'm glad you are so supportive of him. Wouldn't want to see him get the short end of the stick in this set up. You and Buster are such giants. If it was me, I'd be scared out of my mind. Though, I must say, you don't seem scary to me.

SAM: Thank you. I was scary at one time.

ELEANOR: You were?

SAM: Had to be. Boxing. Intimidate them 'til they're up against the ropes. Then suckerpunch them.

ELEANOR: Oh. Sam. Alan and I were having a nice little chat before you arrived.

SAM: (*to Alan*) Oh?

ELEANOR: We were talking about adjustments we wanted made to the script.

SAM: (*to Alan*) Adjustments?

ALAN: No, no ... I wasn't ... there were no adjustments—

SAM: If there's something you're considering.

ALAN: Not at all. You and I have discussed every aspect, every tiny fragment, meticulously, in great and long detail.

SAM: Perhaps too much detail?

ALAN: No.

ELEANOR: I'm sorry, Sam. I didn't mean to imply Alan wanted to make changes. It's not really even changes. Sam, you are a great writer and Alan, as we've established, is a director with great ability. But Buster has made many, many films.

SAM *puts his cards out for* **BUSTER** *who cuts them.*

ACT ONE

Sam: Yes. He has.

Buster *puts his cards out for* **Sam** *who does the same. They begin to lay out cards for double solitaire.*

Eleanor: It would make sense then to use some of his ideas. Having him in the movie. His face is instantly recognizable.
Alan: We don't show the face.

Pause.

Eleanor: What do you mean you don't show the face?
Alan: We don't show it.
Sam: We do in the end.
Alan: Yes.
Eleanor: In the end?
Alan: When we reveal the second character.
Eleanor: I don't understand. Buster's made a career out of his face. How could you not show it?
Alan: Normally his face would, of course, be an asset to a film. Except in this case, it's paramount the face not be shown.
Eleanor: I find it very odd someone would go to all the trouble to engage Buster Keaton, a man famous for his face, to be in a movie and then turn his back to the camera.
Alan: I'm sorry. It is what's required. The face, in this particular instance, is secondary.
Eleanor: Secondary?
Sam: Not secondary, Alan.
Alan: No?
Sam: No. The face is crucial. His face is crucial.
Alan: But the face cannot be seen. The back must be turned.
Sam: Exactly.

Pause.

Alan: Oh, yes. I see what you're saying . . . If we were to take any face and turn it away from the camera, it wouldn't have the same impact. This way, when the face is finally revealed, the experience is much more rewarding. Our idea of who this character is will be transformed in the very moment we see the face.

Sam: More or less . . .

Eleanor: The character. He doesn't even have a name.

Alan: He has a name.

Eleanor: He does?

Alan: Yes. It's—

Buster: O.

Eleanor: O?

Alan: O.

Sam: O.

Eleanor: Oh. I didn't realize that was the name. I thought it was short for something.

Alan: No. Well, yes, it is. In a manner of speaking. O stands for "object," which his character is.

Eleanor: Oh.

Alan: Yes. Then later he plays another character.

Buster: E.

Eleanor: E?

Sam: E.

Alan: E, who is, of course, the subject, the one doing the observing. P.O.V. camera.

Eleanor: Oh.

Buster: No, E.

Alan: Yes. E. For "eye."

Eleanor: Oh. I?

Alan: Yes.

Eleanor: I'm sorry, I thought you said E.

Alan: No. Not I. Eye.

Sam: Eyeball.

Eleanor: Oh.

Buster: No, E.

Eleanor: Oh.

Buster: No. E.

Pause.

ACT ONE

ELEANOR: Oh.
ALAN: Yes. At the end we reveal the subject, E . . .

The YOUNG MAN enters from the parlour, carrying a scotch bottle.

ALAN: . . . to the object.
ELEANOR: Oh.
ALAN: Yes.

ELEANOR turns back to the others, who are completely engaged in playing cards, eating and drinking. The YOUNG MAN pours SAM a refill.

ELEANOR: You've laid out a good hand there, Sam.
SAM: Nothing luckier than having a lady looking over your shoulder.
ELEANOR: Been playing cards long?
SAM: Only as long as I can remember.

The YOUNG MAN offers the cheese plate to SAM.

SAM: Mmm, nibblies. Carry on, Alan. You're doing a bang-up job there.

While ALAN speaks, the others continue to play cards, eat and drink.

ALAN: As I was saying, the character known as E is revealed at the end. But only after O has destroyed all representations of himself. These representations, in the film, come to us in the form of photographs, photographs being slim imitations at best, easy to destroy, to get away from.

The YOUNG MAN offers food to ALAN.

ALAN: No thanks. You see, O—after rocking in the rocking chair for a while—falls asleep and then awakens with a fright. He gets his satchel, pulls out the photos and then tears them up. The tearing up of the photos is of course a metaphor for the act of observation. It is only after he tears up the photos that he is free to actually see himself as he is, and more importantly, how he fears he is.

The **YOUNG MAN** *goes to* **BUSTER**.

ALAN: All this time he's been running away from the eyes: the eyes of the other people, the eyes in the picture, the eyes of the bird in the birdcage and the goldfish . . . And of course the eyes of the other character, the self—or eye, since both E and O will be wearing an eye patch.
ELEANOR: Did you say "eye patch?"
ALAN: To accentuate the eye of both the subject, E and the object—
ELEANOR: Oh.
ALAN: Yes.

ELEANOR *turns back once again to the others.*

ALAN: It is at this point in the film when he realizes he can never get away from himself.

The **YOUNG MAN** *pours a drink for* **BUSTER**. **ALAN** *is becoming more and more passionate about what he is saying.*

ALAN: This is where the nightmare comes in. Jolted awake, the object must face the subject—basically himself. By looking into the dead eye of the subject, he is looking at his final moment. They both are. The object looking into the eye of the subject. And the subject, then, naturally, looking into the eye of the object. Each of them being a reverse of the other.

The others continue to play cards, eat and drink. **BUSTER** *pulls out a cigarette and puts it in his mouth. The* **YOUNG MAN** *tries unsuccessfully to light it.*

ALAN: We must come to terms with the realization we are at once the viewer and the viewed. The subject as well as the object.

ACT ONE

The **Young Man** *continues to try to light* **Buster***'s cigarette, unsuccessfully.*

Alan: One can never be complete if one side does not become engaged with the other. The object must reinvent himself in accordance with the discovery of the subject, become a participant as well as an observer. The self then becomes fully integrated with the viewed self.
Eleanor: Oh.
Alan: Yes.

Pause.

Buster: (*stands*) I think I'll go do the fish now.

The **Young Man** *follows in step behind* **Buster**. **Buster** *tosses the cigarette back behind him as though tossing it away. Without losing step, the* **Young Man** *catches it and puts it his mouth. He lights it, this time successfully and they exit to the parlour, still in unison, closing the door behind them.*

Eleanor: Buster's doing a barbecue. Buster does a great barbecue.
Sam: Oh! A barbecue! I've always wanted to learn how to work one of those.

Sam *opens the parlour door and exits, closing the door behind him.*

Eleanor: I think we'll eat in here. What do you think, Alan?
Alan: Fine. Yes.
Eleanor: Then we won't have to interrupt the card game. Always seems to tie up the parlour when I need it most.
Alan: Card game?
Eleanor: I do hope Sam likes potato salad. I can make coleslaw if you think he'd rather. Myself, I prefer potato salad. Nothing says summer like potato salad.
Alan: You're not going to tell me there's a card game going on right now.

THE STONE FACE

ELEANOR: Don't be silly, Alan. There's always a card game going on.

ELEANOR exits to the parlour, closing the door behind her. **ALAN** *follows her. He tries to open the door but can't because it's stuck. Just then, the* **YOUNG MAN** *enters from the parlour, closing the door behind him. He collects the used glasses. The* **YOUNG MAN***, having collected the glasses, opens the door to exit.*

ALAN: Wait a minute.

The **YOUNG MAN** *stops.*

ALAN: Is this Mr. Beckett's drink?

The **YOUNG MAN** *nods "yes."* **ALAN** *picks up* **SAM***'s drink, sniffs it, looks at it. The* **YOUNG MAN** *exits.* **ALAN** *tries to catch him, but it's too late; the* **YOUNG MAN** *has already closed the door.* **ALAN** *takes a drink from* **SAM***'s glass and makes a sour face as before.*

Blackout.
End of Scene Three.

SCENE FOUR

ALAN *and* **SAM** *watch as* **BUSTER** *tries on a series of identical flattened "porkpie" hats.*

BUSTER: There's this one. Or . . . this one. There's also . . .

He picks up a hat but if "flies" out of his hands. **BUSTER** *takes a step forward to pick up the hat but it moves away from him, seemingly by itself. He takes another step, followed by another and the hat continues to move forward.*
  * **ALAN** *picks up the hat and gives it to* **BUSTER***, who puts it on.*

ACT ONE

BUSTER: . . . this one.
ALAN: You don't understand, Buster. It's not which hat. It's any hat. The hat must hide the face. None of your hats, which are really all identical copies of each other—
BUSTER: (*putting on another hat*) Or this one.

ELEANOR *pokes her head in from the parlour.*

ELEANOR: Buster, would you bring in the garden hose from the front. I need some water for coffee.

ELEANOR *disappears back into the parlour.*

BUSTER: (*switching hats*) How about this one?
ALAN: We can't use any of them. I'm sorry. The hat isn't going to work.

BUSTER *exits to the garden.*

ALAN: When you first suggested Buster for this role I voiced some serious concern.
SAM: You did.
ALAN: Don't get me wrong, I trust your judgment.
SAM: Alan, Everything I envision for the part of O is embodied in this man, Buster Keaton.
ALAN: The thing is, Buster's not the man he once was. To tell you the truth, I don't think he's all there.

BUSTER *enters from the garden pulling a long garden hose behind him. It's up off the ground, which would suggest someone is holding the other end.* **ALAN** *watches the spectacle.* **SAM** *continues to contemplate what* **ALAN** *has just said.* **BUSTER** *exits into the parlour, the hose continuing to move along behind him.*

SAM: Can you be more specific?
ALAN: Sam. Buster is living in a bygone time. He wants things as they were, even if those things interfere with the very essence of the

film itself. And he keeps trying to impose his own ideas. The hat, for example.

SAM *wanders over to the hats, looking them over.*

ALAN: The audience absolutely cannot see the face. And the hat works counter to this. We wouldn't want to destroy the effect of the protagonist having a double. It's such a difficult thing to pull off as it is.

BUSTER *enters from the garden holding the back end of the hose. He exits into the parlour.* **ALAN** *stares after him.*

SAM: I was curious to know which areas of the script Eleanor said needed . . . "adjusting," I think is the word that was bandied about.
ALAN: Sam, Eleanor is hardly the person to consult with on the merits of your writing.
SAM: I'm interested in hearing her thoughts.
ALAN: We were merely using the script as a basis for an argument. A hypothetical discussion.
SAM: Alan, all conversation is hypothetical.
ALAN: Eleanor just meant the making of a film is a relatively new undertaking for us. Whereas for Buster, filmmaking is . . .

SAM *picks up one of* **BUSTER***'s hats and puts it on.*

SAM: Old hat?
ALAN: I suppose you could say that.

SAM *begins to try on a few of the hats while* **ALAN** *continues to explain.*

ALAN: Of course what she's saying is true. Buster is—or rather, was—a skilled filmmaker. No one doubts that. But it was a long time ago. The most he's done lately has been to appear in second-rate beach blanket movies and the occasional television show . . .

ACT ONE

SAM *becomes more and more engrossed with the hats.*

ALAN: Sam. Silent film comedy has certainly informed your work. The relationship between Keaton's work and your own is evident to a partial degree. The Surrealists have claimed Keaton as one of their own. But it is a tenuous relationship at best.

SAM *puts another hat on his head.*

SAM: This one?

ALAN: Your artistry contains threads of similarity. But in actual fact you and Keaton are quite different. As for Eleanor, she's a smart woman, but their brand of comedy is . . . rudimentary.

SAM *puts another hat on his head.*

SAM: This one, I think.

ELEANOR *enters from the parlour, followed by* **BUSTER** *who is holding a pie.*

ELEANOR: I hope you saved room for pie.
SAM: Oh, marvelous. I love pie.
ELEANOR: It's lemon meringue. Squeezed the lemons myself. Had to practically beat the pulp out of them. Under ripe, I think.
SAM: I know what you mean.
ELEANOR: Coffee?
SAM: Let me help you. You can tell me about those adjustments you were talking about.
ALAN: But Sam . . .
SAM: Don't worry, Alan. We're only going to have a little chat. A hypothetical conversation.
ELEANOR: Is there any other kind? (*exiting*) That's a good look for you.
SAM: (*exiting*) You think?

ALAN *turns to* **BUSTER**, *who holds the pie.*

THE STONE FACE

ALAN: Buster. I know you are a filmmaker of extraordinary talent. And I'm only a beginner. For everyone's sake. For the sake of the film . . .

BUSTER *continues to hold the pie.*

ALAN: I've seen and tasted quite a few odd things since coming to this house. And this is all fine and dandy when we're sitting around here talking and so forth. But once we get to New York and start filming . . .

BUSTER *still continues to hold the pie.*

ALAN: I've enjoyed the pranks, the gags. I have. I do have a sense of humour, you know.

Stone-faced, **BUSTER** *continues to hold the pie.*

ALAN: Look. Buster. *Film* is a comedy. But it's a different kind of comedy than you are used to making. Evergreen has commissioned three experimental films from three of the great absurdist playwrights of our time: Ionesco, Pinter, and Sam. This is an artistic endeavour of the utmost seriousness.

BUSTER *raises the pie up slightly.*

BUSTER: Pie?
ALAN: I'm not stupid, you know. I've seen enough silent film comedies to know what's supposed to happen with that pie.

Same position.

BUSTER. Why don't you give it to me?

The invitation is a juicy one.

BUSTER: Never mind. An unfortunate choice of words.

ACT ONE

A moment passes. **BUSTER** *holds the pie out for* **ALAN** *to take, which he does.*

BUSTER: One of the biggest mistakes modern audiences make about silent film comedies. They think everyone threw pies.

SAM *enters from the parlour dragging the front end of the hose along the ground. He crosses the stage, in between* **BUSTER** *and* **ALAN**.

ALAN: I didn't say everyone threw pies.
BUSTER: Not very many silent film comedians threw pies. Except for the Keystone Cops, none of the better-known movies had any pie-throwing at all.
ALAN: I knew that.
BUSTER: When they hired me to do the *Hollywood Cavalcade* television show, they hired me to throw pies. That's the funny thing . . .
SAM: *(from off)* It's stuck. Try lifting it up.
BUSTER: . . . I never threw a pie in my life.

The hose lifts way up, smacking against **ALAN**'s *hand, causing him to put the pie in his own face.*

SAM: *(from off)* That's it! Keep it coming!

The **YOUNG MAN** *enters from the parlour, holding the back end of the hose. The* **YOUNG MAN** *tips his hat to* **ALAN**, *continuing across the stage until he exits out the front door.*

Blackout.
End of Act One.

ACT TWO

SCENE ONE

The film set. The walls are bare.

There is a side table, a rocking chair and also a table and chairs for use when not filming.
   There is a set door and a door resembling a cellar door, or a passageway which could be thought of as a cellar entranceway.
   BUSTER *enters and proceeds to walk across the set, feeling his way along the walls. He seems to be checking his pacing or trying to perfect some sort of walk.*
   ALAN *enters. He holds before him a large diagram consisting of a number of arrows and letters. He walks about the set, inspecting it and consulting the diagram.*
   The two men know the other is in the room, though they are somewhat oblivious to one another. There are times when they may be back to back, circling around one another and other times when they may be walking in the same direction.
   BUSTER, *at some point, follows closely behind* **ALAN**, *causing them to move in unison.*
   They pass the cellar door, and as they do, **ELEANOR** *enters, carrying a basket of apples. She has, in effect, though unintentionally, joined in with the others, as they make their way across the stage.*

THE STONE FACE

ALAN *suddenly notices her, curious as to where she might have come from.*

Meanwhile, **BUSTER** *crosses towards* **ALAN**. *Not noticing him,* **ALAN** *turns and almost crashes into* **BUSTER**.

ALAN *looks at* **BUSTER** *with suspicion.*

SAM *enters through the set door in a fluster, tissues attached to his face. He wears one of* **BUSTER**'s *hats and carries two or three others.*

SAM: Alan, you'll be delighted to hear I've come up with a solution for the hat. Buster. Eleanor.

BUSTER *nods in greeting to* **SAM**.

ALAN: Sam, your face.
SAM: Oh. Yes. Thought I'd save myself a little time and shave on the way over. We were nearing West Eighth. Except it didn't look at all familiar. Then it finally dawned on me you must've said East. The cab driver swung around so quickly I nearly sliced my throat.
ELEANOR: Are you all right?
SAM: Yes. Thank you for asking, Eleanor.

SAM *gives one of the hats to* **ALAN**.

SAM: If you'll put this on.
ALAN: Sam.
SAM: Go on now. Pop it on your head.

SAM *puts the hat on* **ALAN**'s *head.*

SAM: I've been wearing this hat on and off since we left California. There's something about it. I was thinking how distinctly it represents its owner. It delivers us the flavour of Buster Keaton unlike any other prop or clothing item.
ALAN: I agree, Sam. It still doesn't solve the problem of blocking the face.
SAM: No, no. This is what I wanted to show you. Buster, give us your

ACT TWO

handkerchief. It came to me while I was looking for something to clean the blood off the back seat of the cab.

> **Buster** *searches his pockets and pulls out a handkerchief. He gives it to* **Sam**.

Sam: If we put this handkerchief here . . . like this . . .

> **Sam** *puts the handkerchief on* **Buster**'s *head, followed by one of* **Buster**'s *hats.*

Sam: We can use it to block the face and still keep the hat. Buster, if you could move about. You see, Alan, the camera follows like this.

> **Buster** *moves about the room while* **Sam** *and* **Alan** *follow him around as if with a camera.*

Sam: Even when exceeding the forty-five degree angle, the angle of immunity, the face stays hidden. Even when he goes up to cover the mirror. Which wall will the mirror be on?

Alan: *(indicating)* This one here.

> **Buster** *goes to the wall and examines it.*

Alan: Though we will be sliding this wall out for the initial shot.
Sam: Sliding the wall out?
Alan: Yes. It's the beauty of the sound stage, Sam. We can take walls out as need be. Any configuration we need. We'll remove the wall. Position the camera further back to accommodate a wider shot. And then later on, we'll put the wall back for the bit with the mirror. With the wall removed the camera can get a full view of the entire room.
Sam: Oh, I see.

> **Buster** *mimes covering up the "mirror."*

THE STONE FACE

Sam: Yes. You cover the mirror. Yes. Now, it's important we block the face, but we want to maintain the essence of Keaton. The essence of Keaton is now in the wearing of this hat. The hat is a stand-in for the face.

Eleanor: I don't think the hat's enough. If you want Buster Keaton then you have to have at least some kind of gag, otherwise it could be anybody who happens to be wearing a Buster Keaton hat.

*The **Young Man** enters from the "cellar." He is eating an apple and reading a newspaper. He sees the others and is a little startled at the spectacle of all the men in the same hats. Now, of course, there are four. They all look at each other. The **Young Man** folds the newspaper in half and gives it to **Buster**.*

Alan: Wait a minute.

*The **Young Man** stops.*

Alan: Where did you come from?

*The **Young Man** is confused by this question. **Alan** looks or goes towards the "cellar" then shifts his attention to the **Young Man** himself.*

Alan: This is the same fellow I saw at your home in California. Are you an employee of Mr. Keaton's?

*The **Young Man** shakes his head "no."*

Alan: A relative?

*The **Young Man** thinks about this for a moment. The question seems too complicated for him to answer.*

Alan: What's your name?

*The **Young Man** pulls out a business card and gives it to Alan.*

ACT TWO

Alan: Dam—fi—no.

The **Young Man** *tips his hat to* **Alan** *and exits.*

Alan: (*to* **Buster**) Who is he?
Buster: (*shrugging*) Damfino.

Buster *takes the newspaper and unfolds it for reading.*

Sam: I think Eleanor's right. Keaton is the gag. The gag is Keaton. The two are inseparable.

Buster *continues to unfold the paper. He unfolds it more and more, revealing an absurdly large newspaper.*

Sam: The way I see it, the film can only be enhanced by the existence of some form of sight gag. If only to further inform the audience of the essence of Keaton. Something involving grand gestures unfolding in the classic Keaton way.

Buster *has the newspaper almost completely folded out and it covers his whole body. He stands on top of the chair and continues folding it out even more. Even though we can't see his face, by allowing at least the essence of the gag to come through, then we have the essence of Keaton.*
The chair tips over and **Buster** *falls to the floor.*

Eleanor: Buster!

Eleanor *helps* **Buster** *up with* **Alan**'s *assistance.*

Sam: Yes, yes. It's crucial we include a gag. The removal of the dog and cat, I think, will serve us well. It's practically a gag in itself.
Buster: Not yet. But it can be.
Eleanor: Really, Buster. You have to be more careful. You're not supposed to do any more falls.
Buster: It was from a chair, for crying out loud.

THE STONE FACE

ELEANOR: You know what the doctor said.
ALAN: Doctor?
BUSTER: It's nothing.
ELEANOR: Buster has bronchitis.
ALAN: Bronchitis? That can be quite serious, can't it?

BUSTER *pulls out a cigarette and lights up.*

BUSTER: Not if I cut down on the smoking.

ELEANOR *takes the cigarette out of* **BUSTER**'s *mouth and stubs it out.*

ELEANOR: Don't worry. Buster'll have to pace himself is all.
ALAN: That's good to know.
BUSTER: Pace myself? I have a broken bone for every picture I ever made.
ELEANOR: It's true. You can map Buster's career by looking at a set of X-rays.
BUSTER: I did all my own stunts. Not once did I use a double. Walked on top of moving trains making *The General* and *Sherlock Jr.*
ALAN: We want to be careful—
BUSTER: Froze underwater in Lake Tahoe filming *The Navigator.* Almost drowned in the Truckee River for *Our Hospitality.* I broke my ankle making *Electric House*, my neck for *Sherlock Jr.* . . .
ALAN: All right, I understand—you broke your neck?
BUSTER: Yeah. So don't tell me I can't look out for myself. Pace myself. I'm running around with a hankie on my head for chrissakes!

BUSTER *pulls out another cigarette.* **ELEANOR** *takes away the entire pack.*

SAM: Listen, I know what you're going through. My wife subjects me to warm oatmeal on a regular basis. With molasses, no less. I usually manage to throw it out the window when she's not looking—the dog loves it. Sometimes though, I have to put it in my shoe. They mean well, bless them.
BUSTER: Do they?

ACT TWO

ELEANOR: Buster doesn't show it. But he knows how lucky he is. When he married me, I was nothing more than a child bride. The Justice of the Peace found it confusing. He kept trying to marry him to my mother.
BUSTER: That's who that woman was.

ELEANOR gives BUSTER a shove.

SAM: I wonder. Does anyone mind if we stop for lunch? I'm feeling a bit peckish.
ALAN: It's only ten-thirty in the morning.
ELEANOR: Have an apple, Sam. It'll take the edge off.
SAM: *(taking one)* Thanks. Mmm. Yummy.
ELEANOR: Aren't they? I found them in the root cellar.
SAM: You don't say.
ELEANOR: I have some pears here, if you like.
SAM: I'm afraid I'm not much of a pear man.
ALAN: What are you talking about?
SAM: Fruit, Alan.
ELEANOR: Want a pear?
ALAN: What's this about a root cellar?
ELEANOR: The most wonderful discovery. There's potatoes and canned goods. Even jam.
SAM: Really? What kind?
ALAN: No, no, wait a minute. This is a soundstage. This door is put here for authenticity.
ELEANOR: Certainly is authentic.

ELEANOR goes down into the "cellar."

SAM: You don't mind if we take a little break, do you?
ALAN: Sam. This is a soundstage. There is no root cellar.
SAM: But, if there's jam . . .
BUSTER: See if they have any strawberry, would you? Eleanor always buys raspberry jam. I can't stand it. All those little seeds.
SAM: Dentures?
BUSTER: Yeah.

SAM: I know what you mean. The other thing my wife likes to give me is poppy seed cake. It's a real bugger.

SAM *goes down to the "cellar."* **ALAN** *resigns himself. Looks at* **BUSTER**. **ALAN** *sits, takes off his hat.* **BUSTER** *lights up a cigarette.*

ALAN: I thought Eleanor took those away from you.
BUSTER: Always carry back-up.

BUSTER *opens his vest to reveal several packs of smokes. He takes them out, one at a time and slaps them on the table until there's an impressive pile. He removes one last pack from inside his shoe.*

ALAN: Are you sure you should be smoking? With the bronchitis.
BUSTER: Oh that. Eleanor sometimes says things.
ALAN: Says things?
BUSTER: To keep people on their toes. Cranks up the sympathy.
ALAN: What are you saying?
BUSTER: The illnesses change too. Depending on the listener.
ALAN: Buster. Your wife said you had bronchitis.
BUSTER: You're lucky. She tells some people I'm dying. She told one fellow who wanted me for a hemorrhoids commercial I was already dead. Now, if she really wanted to get you, she would have told you I had lung cancer.
ALAN: Lung cancer?
BUSTER: Yeah. That one's real useful around contract negotiations.

BUSTER *takes out cards and begins to shuffle them.*

ALAN: I don't think that's very funny.

BUSTER *is laying cards out for solitaire.*

ALAN: Did you hear what I said?
BUSTER: Yeah. You don't think cancer is funny.
ALAN: Of course I don't. Some things are funny and some things aren't. Even you have to admit to that.

ACT TWO

BUSTER *just looks at him.*

Beat.

BUSTER: I survived a tornado. One of the worst ever. I was only a baby. Thing blew me right outta my crib, sucked me out the window and landed me square in the middle 'a downtown. Mother was looking all over, frantic. There I was, making my way down Angus Street on all fours. Not a mark on me.

Beat.

BUSTER: Do you like magic?
ALAN: Magic?
BUSTER: It's a simple question.
ALAN: Yes. I like magic.
BUSTER: Everyone says they do. Most people don't. Not really.
ALAN: I once held a lady's legs while a magician named Thurston sawed her in half. She slid four inches in my direction. I was almost sick. But I didn't let go. I stayed up all night trying to figure out how he did it.
BUSTER: It was the same for me. Only without the legs. I used to watch Houdini, as a baby, from a steamer trunk in the wings. And then later . . . I watched him from every angle, trying to figure out how he did those magic tricks. Used to drive me crazy. Till one day, I decided he was magic. Then I could see everything.

BUSTER *continues to play cards.*

ALAN: Maybe I seem a bit unbending. I do have a sense of humour.
BUSTER: I think you mentioned that.
ALAN: It's true what I said before. I really do think *The General* was a landmark film. But it was *Sherlock Jr.* I liked. I saw it when I was a kid. Used to always go to the movies. In fact . . . I used to show movies in our attic to the other kids on the block. See I won a contest. In a medical magazine—my parents were both doctors. Whoever could sell the most hypodermic needles won a projec-

tor and a stack of films. The projector was on its last shaky legs. I had to hold it down while I was running it and still the picture shook all over the screen. And the films kept snapping because of the poor quality. I used banana oil to splice them together. That was the thing, apparently: banana oil. Stunk like hell. But it worked. Drove my parents crazy. They never watched any of the films because the projector shook so much the picture hurt my father's eyes. And the smell of the oil. Drove them both mad. I can still smell the stuff.

Pause.

ALAN: Buster. I need to know. Are you going to be okay?

BUSTER: One time me 'n Roscoe played a practical joke involving a turkey.

Beat.

BUSTER: Adolph Zukor was coming to dinner at Roscoe's estate. Zukor was the up and coming big producer of the time. All the greats were there: Mary and Doug, Valentino. Everyone was in on the joke. Except for Zukor. I was to take the part of the hapless servant. I served dinner, making mistake after mistake. I'd take away the soup before people began. I slopped wine all over the table cloth. And every time Roscoe would take me out to the kitchen and give me heck, his voice gettin' louder and louder. By this time, Zukor was becoming more and more uncomfortable until finally the last course was served: turkey. I was supposed to bring it out whole and carve it at the table. I brought it out and displayed it proudly for our guest of honour and then for Roscoe. I brought it closer and closer to Roscoe, tipping it further in his direction until the whole turkey, trimmings and all, landed right on his lap. Roscoe ripped into me like there was no tomorrow, pretending to be angry. Yelling and throwing turkey bits at me. Zukor tried to talk him down, but it was no use. Roscoe took me out to the kitchen and poor Zukor listened to what sounded like a servant getting beaten by his master. Zukor felt so bad for the

ACT TWO

clumsy servant, he kept mumbling to the other guests it didn't matter. And everyone kept commenting on how hard it was to get good help. Roscoe returned from the kitchen to apologize for the inconvenience, cleaning up as he was talking, making a real point of sliding around in a puddle of gravy. Zukor apparently was beside himself and didn't know what to make of it. Meanwhile I was upstairs getting washed and changed. As soon as I came bounding down the stairs and into the dining room, Zukor took one look at me and had it all figured out. Well we all had a good laugh and sat down to eat.

ALAN: So you're telling me everything will be fine?

BUSTER: Yeah. Roscoe had another turkey in the oven.

ALAN: Of course.

Pause.

BUSTER: I didn't wear a disguise. Didn't have to. I was at the height of my career then. Everyone knew my face. But no one expected me to be serving a nine course meal. And people generally see what they expect to see. It's something else Roscoe taught me. Zukor knew my face. He'd just arrived in town and wanted to meet me. But my face inches away from him, pouring wine—he didn't see it.

Pause.

BUSTER: We see what we want to see.

BUSTER exits through the set door, closing it behind him. ALAN sits for a moment. He goes to follow BUSTER out the door, but can't. The door is stuck. ALAN thinks for a moment. Just then, SAM comes up from the "cellar" carrying an armload of jam.

SAM: Look, Alan. All strawberry! Not a raspberry seed in sight!

Blackout.
End of Scene One.

THE STONE FACE

Scene Two

The film set as before.
The table and chairs are gone. The rocking chair and side table remain. The wall referred to earlier by **Alan** *is now missing. The missing wall has part of it still intact on the sides and top and a little threshold of sorts on the bottom. In effect, the emptiness that is the missing wall, has a frame.* **Buster** *as O enters. He wears a heavy overcoat and his signature hat with the handkerchief underneath.* **Buster** *is followed by* **Sam***, who wears his Buster Keaton hat. Following behind* **Sam** *is* **Alan***, who carries the diagram. Following* **Alan** *is the* **Young Man***, who carries two folded blankets.* **Buster** *closes and locks the door, the others continuing to follow behind. He then checks his pulse, the others looking on. The* **Young Man** *deposits the blankets beside the rocking chair and then exits, all the while taking note of the curious goings-on.* **Buster** *turns around again and begins to walk across the room, the others continuing behind him.*

Sam: Good. Let's try it again. Only turn in even more.

Buster *nods then exits.*

Alan: Sam, I think I should give the directions.
Sam: Yes, yes, of course. But lift those gams, Alan. We haven't got all day.

Sam *exits, followed by* **Alan** *who checks the door and the frame on his way out. He closes the door behind him.* **Buster** *enters again. This time* **Alan** *is behind him, with* **Sam** *following behind* **Alan***. Also following behind is the* **Young Man***, who carries an animal basket.* **Buster** *closes the door, locks it, checks his pulse as before then continues moving across the stage, only walking sideways.* **Alan** *and* **Sam** *continue behind him. The* **Young Man** *moves toward his intended destination, once again, taking note of the actions of the others.*

ACT TWO

SAM: Yes. Now. This is where you turn.

Still holding the animal basket, the **YOUNG MAN** *turns towards the others.*

ALAN: Yes, this is where you . . .

BUSTER *turns.*

ALAN: . . . turn.

The **YOUNG MAN** *turns again. He begins to sidestep towards his destination.*

SAM: Pause.

BUSTER *stops. The* **YOUNG MAN**, *taking his cue from* **BUSTER**, *also stops.*

SAM: And . . .
ALAN: React.

The **YOUNG MAN** *doesn't know what to do.*

BUSTER: What am I reacting to?
ALAN: The incongruity of size.

The **YOUNG MAN** *is totally baffled.* **BUSTER** *turns to* **SAM** *for interpretation.*
SAM: The little dog and the big cat.
ALAN: One normally expects a large dog and a small cat. It's counter to expectation.
BUSTER: Uh huh.
ALAN: The incongruity element, when it works against the inherent order of things, can be really quite . . . well . . . funny.

BUSTER *and the* **YOUNG MAN** *look at* **ALAN**.

ALAN: See, we put them side by side—
BUSTER: The funny animals.
ALAN: Yes. The animals will be side by side in front of you. They'll be in a basket.

*The **YOUNG MAN** clues in: the basket! He puts the basket down in its location. He then pulls out a banana and begins to peel it.*

ALAN: You react.
BUSTER: Because they're so funny.
ALAN: Yes.
BUSTER: When do I react to their eyes?
ALAN: Do one right after the other.
BUSTER: One eye?
ALAN: One reaction.
BUSTER: So I react twice?
ALAN: Yes. The first reaction is to the size and the second reaction is to the eyes.
BUSTER: How will they know the difference?
ALAN: The animals?
BUSTER: The audience.
ALAN: They'll know because you will be turning their heads away.
BUSTER: The audience?
ALAN: The animals. When you see them looking at you, you avert their eyes by turning their heads.
BUSTER: I still don't see how the audience is going to know the difference.
ALAN: Look, just react once to the size, then again to the eyes. Like this.

***ALAN** demonstrates two reactions. The **YOUNG MAN** looks alarmed.*

SAM: It's a little much, don't you think?
ALAN: Well, not exactly like that.
SAM: I hope not.
ALAN: Never mind. React twice. We'll figure it out in editing.
BUSTER: Never heard that one before.

ACT TWO

The **YOUNG MAN** *nods in amusement, understanding all about editing.* **ALAN** *sees the* **YOUNG MAN** *is smug. The* **YOUNG MAN** *backs away.*

ALAN: Just so you know . . . the use of banana peels in comedy has long outworn its welcome.

The **YOUNG MAN** *exits, confused, eating his banana.* **ALAN** *shows the diagram to* **BUSTER**. **SAM** *looks on.*

ALAN: Here we have the arrows indicating the movement of the various participants. "D" is for dog and "C" is for—
BUSTER: Cat?
ALAN: Yes.
BUSTER: My one day of formal schooling finally paid off.
ALAN: Now, O starts here.
BUSTER: Where the dog is.
ALAN: No, this is the door. The arrow indicates . . .
BUSTER: That I'm walking this way.
ALAN: No, no. This is the arrow for the cat.

BUSTER *takes the diagram to have a better look. It's awkward and he's not sure how it should be held.* **ALAN** *turns it around for him, but* **BUSTER** *manages to get the thing turned around again.* **ALAN** *corrects him.*

ALAN: Like this. After you react to the eyes you go to big D, back to C, then to D. D moves in this direction back to where C was.

BUSTER *twists the diagram around again.*

ALAN: Reaction from O at seeing C. Now D back to the C position. Reaction . . .

ALAN *takes the diagram from* **BUSTER**.

ALAN: Let's move on, shall we?

THE STONE FACE

SAM: Good idea. All right. Now, Buster. Starting with the cat . . .

> **BUSTER** *mimes picking up the "cat."*

ALAN: *(consulting the diagram)* It says here he starts with the dog.

> **BUSTER** *mimes picking up the "dog".*

SAM: The cat, I think.

> **BUSTER** *pauses, holding two mimed animals up, waiting for a decision to be made.*

ALAN: Are you sure?
SAM: Yes. Cats are much funnier.

> **BUSTER** *mimes putting the "dog" back in the basket, continuing to hold the "cat."* **SAM** *takes the diagram from* **ALAN**.

SAM: I think we can safely dispense with this.
ALAN: It's your diagram.
SAM: It is? Oh yes. So it is.

> **SAM** *rolls up the diagram and puts it aside.*

SAM: Right. Now starting with the cat.

> **BUSTER** *begins the routine, taking the "cat" to the door.*

SAM: Putting it out the door . . .

> *He opens the door, puts the "cat" out, closes the door.*

SAM: Good. So you come back for the dog . . .

> **BUSTER** *returns to the basket, retrieves the "dog," goes back to the set door, opens it and puts the "dog" out.*

ACT TWO

SAM: And once it's outside . . .

> *The* **YOUNG MAN** *enters through the open door, carrying a goldfish bowl, which is filled with water.* **BUSTER** *closes the door with the* **YOUNG MAN** *now inside.* **BUSTER** *goes back to the basket . . . reacts . . .*

SAM: The cat comes back . . . good . . .

> **BUSTER** *continues with the act.*
>
> *In the meantime, the* **YOUNG MAN** *moves towards the side table with the goldfish bowl.*

ALAN: Can you slow it down please, Buster?

> **BUSTER** *looks at* **ALAN**. *The* **YOUNG MAN** *looks at* **ALAN** *also.* **BUSTER** *then begins to move in slow motion. He will continue to perform the routine, repeating the actions as needed. Following* **BUSTER**'s *lead, the* **YOUNG MAN** *moves in slow motion as well, making his way towards the table with the goldfish bowl, where he will eventually deposit it and move back towards the set door to exit.*

ALAN: Sam. I realize this is a collaboration. And you are the main creative force.
SAM: Don't underestimate your contribution, Alan. You are the interpreter. The intermediary. Do you know if there's any coffee?
ALAN: Could you stop please, Buster?

> **BUSTER** *stops. The* **YOUNG MAN** *continues for a few moments and then, following* **BUSTER**'s *lead, he too stops.* **ALAN** *takes note of* **BUSTER** *and the* **YOUNG MAN**, *who stand motionless, still holding the goldfish bowl.*

ALAN: Sam. Perhaps we should take this conversation elsewhere.
SAM: We are pressed for time. Resume please, Buster.

THE STONE FACE

BUSTER *and the* **YOUNG MAN** *resume.*

ALAN: Stop please.

They stop.

ALAN: I understand film is a new medium for you—
SAM: For you too. Resume.

They resume.

ALAN: Yes, of course for me too. I meant for both of us. It's just . . . I guess I'm not used to working quite this way . . .
SAM: What way?

ALAN *observes* **BUSTER** *opening the door while the* **YOUNG MAN** *exits through it, both continuing to move in slow motion. No sooner does* **BUSTER** *close the door than it is opened again.*
  ALAN *watches as the* **YOUNG MAN** *enters, this time carrying a birdcage. The* **YOUNG MAN** *proceeds to move towards the side table, all the while continuing to move in slow motion.*

SAM: Buster. I don't feel you're quite getting what I mean here by slower.

BUSTER *and the* **YOUNG MAN** *look at* **ALAN**, *and then they slow down their actions even more!*

ALAN: Sam. You and I have always maintained a close working relationship. It's a relationship I value most highly.

BUSTER *and the* **YOUNG MAN** *continue at the same ridiculously slow pace.*

SAM: Alan. Perhaps it's the very fact of it being film that's got you so bothered. You've always begun each project by building from the ground up. This should be no different.

ACT TWO

BUSTER *and the* **YOUNG MAN** *are still continuing with their actions.*

ALAN: Stop please, Buster.

BUSTER *and the* **YOUNG MAN** *stop.*

ALAN: What I meant by slower is you have to leave a gap in the action. Not slow it down entirely. O has to have time to see the animals come back into the room. So when the audience sees them—
BUSTER: Wait a minute. I see the animals before the audience does?
ALAN: Yes.
BUSTER: No, no, no. You can't have your main character ahead of your audience.
ALAN: Why not?
BUSTER: This is film. They'll see it as a trick. It'll be the death of you.

BUSTER *removes his hat and his handkerchief and puts them down.*

BUSTER: Say you have a banana peel.
ALAN: Banana peel?

The **YOUNG MAN** *pulls a banana peel out of his pocket and offers it to* **ALAN** *who rejects it.*

BUSTER: Yes. You show the banana peel lying on the ground.

The **YOUNG MAN** *puts the peel on the ground.*

BUSTER: You show your main character walking towards the peel. Only instead of tripping on it, you have him pick it up . . .

BUSTER *picks up the peel.*

BUSTER: . . . and march off.

Alan: This isn't about banana peels.
Buster: Alan. It's always about banana peels.
Sam: Buster is using the banana peel as a metaphor.
Alan: Yes, I think I know that.
Buster: I made a movie once called *The High Sign*. It was my first two-reeler. I delayed its release because I didn't want the film to mark me. Because I cheated my audience. I had my character see the banana peel, pick it up, give the "high sign" and walk off. End of film. Thumbed my nose up at them. Never did it again. See, it's okay to fool your character. But never your audience.
Alan: But then all you're doing is playing out a prediction.
Buster: That's right. The banana peel speaks for itself.
Sam: The banana peel is its own shorthand in the language of comedy.
Buster: Yes. But you always have to look for the twist.
Sam: Play with their expectations.
Buster: Yes. Take *Sherlock Jr.*
Sam: Yes, yes, *Sherlock Jr.* You see Alan, how it goes is, the projectionist—the boy—has entered into the film to become Sherlock. Ward Crane, who plays Sherlock's rival, comes by to court Sherlock's girl. If I may ... (*taking the peel from* **Buster**) Ward gives Sherlock a banana and sends him into the other room to get rid of him while he takes the girl into the parlour.

Sam *acts out the scene. The* **Young Man** *looks on intently, impressed perhaps.*

Sam: Sherlock eats the banana. He puts the peel on the ground ...

Sam *throws the peel on the ground.*

... waiting for Crane to come into the living room and trip. Sherlock keeps trying to get him to come closer—it's the funniest thing—Ward keeps coming closer. Still he misses the peel. He goes back to the dining room to make love to the girl. Meanwhile Sherlock, in his anger, forgets all about the peel and charges in after them. And so ...
Alan: He trips on the peel.

ACT TWO

Sam: Yes. The audience knows what's going to happen. But they almost can't believe it when it does.
Buster: Because it's not about surprise. It's about expectation.
Sam: Well put.
Buster: Thank you.

The **Young Man** *picks up the peel and puts it in his pocket.*

Sam: Of course, it's obvious, Alan. O mustn't see the animals before the audience. It's the reverse of everything we've done.
Alan: So we don't cut away.
Buster: No. You stick with the wide shot. Your wide shot will cement the pace and give the audience full view of the routine.
Sam: Yes, yes. Good.

The **Young Man** *notices the missing wall. He finds it curious and tries to figure out what it is.* **Alan** *looks on.*

Sam: So expecting something is the same as—
Buster: . . . being surprised by it. You're just looking at it from the other side.
Sam: Then it's useless for him to try to change anything.
Buster: He has to try. This is the struggle. The gag gives him everything he needs.
Sam: The gag is a reflection of his predicament.

Reflection! The **Young Man** *surmises the missing wall must be a mirror. He reacts accordingly.*

Buster: Only he doesn't know it. At least not yet.

Alan *becomes distracted from the conversation. He moves closer to the* **Young Man**, *looking on intently.*

Sam: The removal of the cat and dog, similarly the covering up of the fish bowl and the birdcage to avert the eyes of the pets.
Buster: And the mirror.

THE STONE FACE

Sam: Yes. The blocking of the reflection.

*The **Young Man** covers his eyes so as not to see his "reflection." He slowly uncovers his eyes and looks at himself.*

Sam: Every action illustrates the theme. Like having one routine on top of another.
Buster: That's right.
Sam: In order for it to play, the main character has to be behind the entire time.
Buster: Until the end.
Sam: When he finally meets his fate.

*The **Young Man** then steps into the "reflection," thus breaking the illusion. He turns, facing **Alan**.*

Buster: Doesn't have any choice.

*The **Young Man** pulls the banana peel from his pocket and offers it to **Alan**.*

Sam: He must accept it.

*This time **Alan** takes the peel.*

Buster: It's the only way.
Sam: If he wants to become one with himself. He must transcend.

*Putting the peel in his pocket, **Alan** notices the **Young Man** mimicking his actions.*

Buster: First he must see.
Sam: To be is to be perceived.

*The **Young Man** turns away.*

Buster: To be perceived is to be.

ACT TWO

ALAN *turns away.*

SAM: Yes.

ALAN *and the* **YOUNG MAN** *turn back towards each other at the same time. They continue the game by moving about in unison.*

BUSTER: Like your O fellow finally looking at your E fellow . . .
SAM: Yes.
BUSTER: Who's been looking all along at the O fellow . . .
SAM: Who, up until the end, has been running from E. . . only to realize . . .
BUSTER: He can never get away.
SAM: Exactly. Did you get that, Alan?

ALAN *looks at* **SAM**.

SAM: Good. Very good.

SAM *and* **BUSTER** *exit.* **ALAN** *turns his attention back to the* **YOUNG MAN**. *The* **YOUNG MAN** *tips his hat, but* **ALAN** *doesn't have one.*

ALAN *goes to where* **BUSTER**'s *hat is and picks it up, and as he does so, the* **YOUNG MAN** *"disappears."* **ALAN** *goes back to the "mirror" only to find the* **YOUNG MAN** *is no longer there.* **ALAN** *looks on either side of the frame, but can't figure out where the* **YOUNG MAN** *has gone. He turns away from the missing wall while putting the hat on his head. Suddenly, the frame surrounding the missing wall falls forward around* **ALAN**.

Blackout.
End of Scene Two.

THE STONE FACE

Scene Three

Film *and projection "booth."*

Film *is the set without any walls. The door, however, remains as does the rocking chair, the side table, the birdcage and the goldfish bowl.*

The **Young Man** *enters, sets up the projector and runs* Film. *Once it begins, he falls asleep.* **Buster**, *as O, enters through the set door, back to the audience, carrying a briefcase. He seems to be running away from something. He closes and locks the door, takes his pulse, crosses the set with his back to the audience. He sits in the rocking chair facing away from the audience and rocks. He suddenly stops rocking and, fearfully, he goes to the birdcage and covers it up with one of the blankets. He returns to the rocking chair, rocks, stops, stands, then covers up the goldfish bowl with the other blanket. He returns to the rocking chair and resumes rocking once again.*

He stops again, pulls out a photo from his briefcase and tears it up. He pulls out another and then tears it up too. He resumes rocking and then falls asleep.

Buster *and the* **Young Man** *are simultaneously jolted awake as if by a nightmare.* **Buster** *stands and turns to face the audience. He wears an eye patch. He has a look of sheer horror on his face. The* **Young Man** *approaches him and looks at his face. He too displays a look of horror. The two men slowly raise their hands in unison and cover their eyes.*

The lights slowly fade.
End of Scene Three.

ACT TWO

Scene Four

On a bench outside a cinema in New York.

As well as the bench, there is also a small table, a door on a frame, and a crate on wheels. Situated directly behind the crate, is a sign. The sign reads:

New York Film Festival
presents
Film

Buster sits, playing cards and smoking. **Alan** paces.

Alan: How do we know it's a vicious dog?
Buster: He's barking.
Alan: Maybe he's happy to see him.
Buster: You're complicating things.
Alan: Does he climb through a window?
Buster: The dog's on the porch, Alan. Pay attention.
Alan: I don't hear anything.
Buster: It's a silent film.

Alan continues to pace.

Buster: You decided not to go in. There's no use dwelling on what might be happening.
Alan: Why didn't you go?
Buster: I never go to my screenings.
Alan: What time is it?
Buster: It's almost ten. Esther's father is almost home.
Alan: No. I mean, what time is it?

Buster looks at his watch.

THE STONE FACE

Buster: They haven't started yet. We're about three minutes to opening credits.

Buster takes a drag from his cigarette.

Alan: Do you think I could get one of those?
Buster: I didn't know you smoked.
Alan: Only in times of terror.

Buster pulls out a packet of smokes and a rosary from his pant pockets. He puts the rosary down and gives Alan a cigarette. Alan notices the rosary.

Alan: Oh. You're Catholic.
Buster: Only in times of terror.

Alan continues to pace.

Buster: Would you sit down? You're making me nervous.
Alan: I don't know how you can be so calm.
Buster: There are benefits in coming to the end of one's life.

Alan stops pacing and looks at Buster.

Buster: The dog's still on the front porch, Alan.

Alan sits down and absentmindedly picks up the rosary.

Alan: Does he call someone?
Buster: There's no time.
Alan: Does he go out the back door?
Buster: No. The dog can run faster than he can.
Alan: Oh.

Pause.

Alan: How does the dog know?

ACT TWO

Buster *is engrossed in his cards.*

Buster: Hmm?
Alan: How does the dog know he's gone round the back?
Buster: The dog has sharp teeth. It doesn't matter how he knows.

Alan, *realizing what he's holding, puts the rosary down.*

Alan: Does he toss a piece of meat out onto the porch? With a drug of some kind buried in it. Or maybe the meat's gone bad.
Buster: Alan. There's nothing funny about a dead dog.
Alan: Okay, okay.

Alan *stands, begins to pace.* **Buster** *continues playing cards. The* **Young Man** *enters from a location other than the cinema door. He goes to the cart, tries to move it, but it's stuck. The* **Young Man** *exits.*

Alan: I still don't hear anything.
Buster: Relax, Alan. Worrying isn't going to change anything. If there's one thing I've learned, it's this: Gotta be prepared. I always have a deck of cards with me. I got a deck of cards in one pocket and a rosary in the other. This way, when I die, no matter which direction I'm headed for, I'm prepared.

Buster *puts the rosary in his pocket.*

Buster: You never know what cards you're going to get dealt. Sometimes you get a good hand and other times . . . you find yourself playing second fiddle to Jimmy Durante. Imagine me, a straight man. I gave 'em straight. I played all my scenes with the zeal of a wet dish rag. People think it was sound did me in. That wasn't it. 'Less you count the sound of my career being crushed under the studio bosses' heels. They told me—Chaplin, Lloyd— told me working for MGM would be a mistake. And it was. Biggest of my life. They gave me my own bungalow. Consolation prize, I guess. Everything was glass. Hurt my eyes to look at it.

Pause.

BUSTER: He's a short man, you know.
ALAN: Thalberg?
BUSTER: Shorter'n me. Takes all his meetings sitting down. Short man. Short letters. "You are hereby notified for good and sufficient cause, we hereby terminate the contract with you dated October fifth, nineteen thirty-two." I took a baseball bat to all that glass. Shattered every pane of it.

Pause.

BUSTER: How 'bout you, Schneider? Those letters you sent to those producers. Giving them fifty percent of everything. What happened? Anyone own you?

ALAN *sits and absentmindedly turns a card over.* **BUSTER** *plays it.*

ALAN: I sent out sixty letters and I got two responses. One was "no thanks." The other was from Billy Rose. It said "Be at the Ziegfeld Theatre on Sixth Avenue, two o'clock, Thursday. I don't have much time."

ALAN *plays another card or two.*

ALAN: All I could see poking out from Billy's desk was Billy's cigar. His voice was like a high-pitched fog horn, cutting through the smoke. He had exactly four words for me. "Kid," he said—I was thirty—"Don't do it." Then he stood, raising his full diminutive self, and repeated the last three words: "Don't do it." Then he left the room. I guess Billy was looking out for my millions. It was good advice. Even though he still didn't offer me a job.

Faint laughter is heard from off. **ALAN** *jumps up.*

ALAN: What was that?

ACT TWO

Faint laughter is heard again.

ALAN: Sounds like laughter.
BUSTER: That's good, isn't it?
ALAN: Yeah. I didn't expect quite so much of it.

The **YOUNG MAN** *enters with a toolkit. He begins to work on the cart, pulling out and trying various tools, including a hammer.*
Laughter is heard once again. **ELEANOR** *comes rushing in, followed by* **SAM**.

ELEANOR: Buster, you'll never guess. They're showing *Cops*. They're laughing at *Cops*. They love it.
ALAN: What's going on?
SAM: They're screening a few of Buster's short films before they show *Film*.
ELEANOR: They're laughing, Buster. They haven't forgotten. They're laughing. Come when you're ready, Alan.
SAM: Don't be too long. The best part's coming up.

ELEANOR *and* **SAM** *exit to the cinema. The* **YOUNG MAN**, *having finished his task, wheels the cart off the stage, leaving behind the toolkit. The crate was actually blocking part of the Film Festival sign. The sign now reads:*

NEW YORK FILM FESTIVAL

PRESENTS

FILM

STAR

BUSTER KEATON

Attached to the sign is a framed photo of a young Buster Keaton, the same photo as was seen in Act One. More faint laughter is heard from off.

Buster: Laughter. What d'ya know?
Alan: The audience. After seeing your films. They'll be disappointed.
Buster: They won't be.

Pause.

Alan: How about you? Are you disappointed?
Buster: I was just in a film called *How to Stuff a Wild Bikini*. How could I be disappointed?

Alan *waits.*

Buster: I'm not disappointed. You made a good film. It's better than good: it's Beckett.
Alan: And Keaton.

Pause.

Buster: And Schneider.

Pause.

Buster: Besides, if the audience doesn't like it, we can always turn their heads away.

A shared joke. **Alan** *wanders over to the photo.*

Alan: All those films. You never cracked a smile.

Buster *wanders over as well.*

Buster: They used to call me the human mop. Mopped up the floor with me. Had a handle sewn right into my costume so they could throw me around better. That was the act: me getting tossed around. "The Three Keatons" we was billed as. Had to dress me up as a midget to avoid the child welfare people. They wanted to shut us down. One night my father threw me right out into the

ACT TWO

audience. I was out cold for eighteen hours straight. If only Houdini had seen that. Now there was a buster.

Pause.

Buster: Some guys. They can mug it up. Not me. If I smile, the humour's gone. My father knew it. Soon as I smiled, I got a whack on the back of the head. It's how he rehearsed me. You learn good that way.
Alan: Hard luck.

Buster *removes the photo from the sign.*

Buster: Never did make it off the old nitrate stock. Dissolved into nothing. The only thing left is this photograph.

Buster *gives the photo to* **Alan**. *The* **Young Man** *enters, picks up the sign and exits.* **Buster** *wanders back to the card game.*

Buster: I was born in Piqua, Kansas. On a stopover in the Traveling Medicine Show. There was a cyclone blew through there the day I was born. Town was wiped clear off the map. I was born in a place that doesn't exist.

Pause.

Buster: Give up?
Alan: What?
Buster: The dog. Give up?
Alan: Never.

Alan *goes back to sit on the bench. He puts down the photograph.*

Alan: The dog is directly on the other side of the door?
Buster: Yes.

77

BUSTER *turns another card over, gives it to* ALAN, *who plays it.*

BUSTER: You've just answered your own question.

ALAN *looks at him, not understanding.*

BUSTER: Houdini's last exit. "It's right there in front of your eyes," he'd say. "The solution is the same as the problem. Just gotta turn it around."
ALAN: Turn it around?
BUSTER: Review the details. Red Skelton is trapped alone inside a house he's not supposed to be in. Only he can't leave because there's a vicious dog on the other side of the door waiting to rip him to shreds. He's tried wearing Esther Williams' clothes to fool the dog. But it's not working and Esther's father is due to come home at ten o'clock. Skelton's on one side of the door and the dog's on the other side. Which is exactly where he would want the dog to be: on the other side.
ALAN: Yes, but he has to be on the other side of the door too.
BUSTER: No. He has to be on this side of the door. It's the door that has to change. Then everything else will change too. He takes the door off its frame and turns it around. And when he does, the dog comes into the house. The dog is now on the inside. While Skelton is on—
ALAN: The outside.

Pause.

ALAN: *Sherlock Jr.* The part where the young man falls asleep in the projection room and then enters right into the film. The transition is virtually seamless. It's hard to tell: did you have actors on stage for this sequence. Or was it only film?
BUSTER: *Film?*
ALAN: Yes, I—(*gets it*) . . . *Film.*
BUSTER: Red Queen.
ALAN: (*cards*) Oh.

ACT TWO

Alan *plays the card.* **Buster** *gathers the cards up, stands.* **Alan** *stands also.* **Buster** *gives the cards to* **Alan.**

Buster: Gonna call in all bets. Recoup my losses. It's the right thing to do, isn't it?
Alan: Yes. Yes it is.

The **Young Man** *enters again. He picks up the bench* **Alan** *and* **Buster** *were sitting on and exits.*

Buster: Not going to be easy. (*shouting*) Thalberg!—and don't tell him I said this—he's a damn good poker player.
Alan: Maybe (*shouting*) Thalberg!'s just lucky.
Buster: Don't knock luck. I used to have some of it. Not to worry. He might have the luck. But I got the face.

Buster exits through the door. **Alan** *picks up the photo, looks at it.*

The **Young Man** *enters. He picks up the small table and exits.*

Alan *is still holding the photo. He turns it around and, noticing the sticky paper attached to the back, removes it. The paper sticks to his hand.*

Delighted, he puts his hand to the ground and steps on the paper with his shoe. Then, hearing the **Young Man** *approach, he puts his foot out, waiting.*

The **Young Man** *enters, stepping on the sticky paper, which, of course, sticks to his shoe. Annoyed, he shakes his foot to try to remove it.*

Alan *hands the* **Young Man** *the photo. The* **Young Man** *exits, shaking his foot as he goes.* **Alan** *approaches the door. He goes to open the door, hesitates, and then tries it. But it's stuck.* **Alan** *sees the toolkit. He goes to it. The* **Young Man** *enters. He too goes to the toolkit.* **Alan** *and the* **Young Man** *face each other. The* **Young Man** *opens the toolkit.* **Alan**, *takes out a hammer, goes to the door and begins to work on it. The* **Young Man**, *in the meantime, closes the lid to the toolkit, picks it up and exits.*

Alan *turns back to see the* **Young Man** *is gone. He looks about* *him, noticing there's nothing left but him and the door. He removes the door from its hinges. He then turns the door around.* **ALAN** *is now on the other side.*

The **YOUNG MAN** *enters, picks up the door and frame and removes it, leaving* **ALAN** *alone on stage, back to the audience.*

ALAN *exits.*

The stage is bare.

Silence.

Blackout.
End of Play.